DATE			

BAKER & TAYLOR

Illustrated History of
MARTIAL ARTS

AIKIDO

by Jerry Craven

illustrated by Jean Dixon

THE ROURKE CORPORATION, INC.
VERO BEACH, FL 32964

PHOTO CREDITS

Photography by Kevin Casey

Library of Congress Cataloging-in-Publication Data

Craven, Jerry.
      Aikido / by Jerry Craven.
        p. cm. — (Illustrated history of martial arts)
      Includes index.
      ISBN 0-86593-364-2
      1. Aikido—Juvenile literature. [1. Aikido.] I. Title.
II. Series.
GV1114.35.C73   1994
796.8'154—dc20   94-4093
                                            CIP

Printed in the USA   AC

TABLE OF CONTENTS

1

ORIGINS OF

A
I
K
I
D
O

Aikido is a new martial art. At the same time, it is ancient in that the founder of aikido, Morihei Ueshiba, created it from older forms. The most important of the older arts Morihei drew upon are *jujitsu* and *kendo,* or Japanese sword fighting.

As a young man, Morihei learned how to use a sword from Sokaku Takeda, the best sword fighter in Japan. The sword art Morihei learned dates from the 12th century, and was developed by the Takeda family. It remained a family secret of the Takeda clan for hundreds of years.

Morihei did not introduce the sword into aikido. He did, though, adapt some of the circular motions from the Takeda sword fighting system. Also, he claimed to replace the sword of war with a sword of the mind. By this he meant that an aikidoist would concentrate on cutting out everything bad within the self. By "bad" he meant everything harmful to *ai*, or harmony – things like vanity, hate and the desire to hurt others.

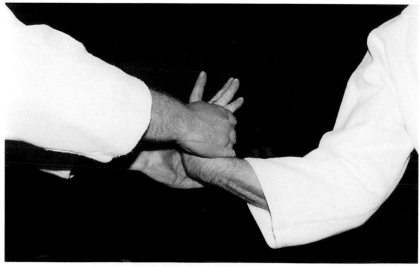

Aikidoists learn hand locks as a way to stop an attacker.

Aikido emphasizes circular movements.

From jujitsu, he took various techniques of applying pressure to joints in order to stop an attacker.

Morihei also introduced ancient techniques of fighting with a stick or staff into aikido self-defense.

2 AIKIDO AND THE OTHER MARTIAL ARTS

Aikido is different from all other martial arts. It is unique in many ways.

Aikido is a recent martial art, developed in the 20th century by Master Morihei Ueshiba in Japan. Some of the techniques are old, for the master adapted much from the samurai warrior tradition.

Aikido does not teach how to attack. The fighting techniques are only for self-defense.

Aikido teaches that it is necessary to care about an attacker. Aikido presents ways to overcome an attacker without causing anyone serious injury. One who attacks an aikidoist will experience pain but will not be permanently hurt.

There are no aikido contests, competitions or tournaments.

Aikido teaches that everyone has *ki,* a form of inner energy that all creatures share. This energy is focused at the center of gravity in the human body, two inches below the navel.

Aikido teaches how to fall as part of the strategy of overcoming an attack. For an aikidoist, a fall is not a sign of defeat. It is a deliberate act to prevent self-injury and to move toward a better position for self-defense in a fight.

Aikido movements are circular. The basic strategy of aikido involves smooth, oval or circular movements. An aikidoist meets an attacker with open hands and smooth, dancelike motions of the hands, body and feet. The circular motion helps maintain the aikidoist's balance and aids in causing an attacker to lose balance.

People not trained in how to fall can suffer serious injury. Landing as illustrated here (on head or knee or elbow) can cause permanent injury. Aikido teaches techniques for falling without being hurt.

3

THE

M
E
A
N
I
N
G

OF
AIKIDO

An important goal in aikido is to blend body and mind through careful training. For an aikido master, self-defense is secondary. Some refer to the mental training as "spiritual" because of the emphasis on inner peace, harmony with creative powers, and proper behavior.

In the middle of the Japanese word "aikido" is the term "ki." There are many ways to define ki. It is a form of power. Some like to think of ki as the creative power in the universe. Others call it the life energy that is in all people, though few are aware of it.

The founder of aikido taught that ki is linked to breath. To learn to use ki, then, it is important to learn techniques for breathing and controlling breath.

Aikido masters who learned the founder's methods teach that ki has its focus in a particular spot in the human body. The spot is two inches below the navel. Another term for that place is the "center of gravity." To control the focus of ki, then, means to control the balance of the body.

The term *ai* means "the way" or "the path," and *do* means "harmony." Put the three terms together, and you have "aikido," or "the way of harmony with ki."

These front and side views show proper stance in aikido. Here, the master wears a hakima, *a full-cut pair of trousers worn over the traditional white martial arts uniform. Aikido borrowed the hakima from the uniform of Japanese sword fighters.*

4

THE MAN WHO BEGAN AIKIDO:

EARLY LIFE

The founder of aikido, Morihei Ueshiba, was small and weak as a child. He liked studying mathematics and philosophy. His father encouraged him to become stronger by learning sumo wrestling. When a gang of criminals beat up his father, Morihei began to work at developing his body, thinking he needed to be strong to defend himself. He learned later that it was more important to know techniques for self-defense than to be physically powerful.

As a teenager, Morihei worked as a teacher in an abacus school, then as a clerk in a tax office.

The Japanese army refused him because he was half an inch too short. Morihei wanted to be in the army, so he tried to make himself taller. He did some odd stretching exercises, such as hanging from the branches of trees with weights strapped to his legs.

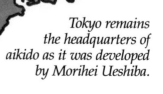

Tokyo remains the headquarters of aikido as it was developed by Morihei Ueshiba.

Master Morihei Ueshiba could disarm a swordsman by using only a folded fan as a weapon.

When he again tried to enlist, the army took him in spite of his height, which was just over five feet. He served for four years, including some combat missions in Manchuria during the Russo-Japanese War of 1904-1905.

After his military service, Morihei took up the study of jujitsu in a serious way. He later used jujitsu as part of the basis for aikido.

5

THE FOUNDER OF AIKIDO:

MATURE YEARS

After his military service, Morihei Ueshiba worked as a lumberjack, as a security guard and as a teacher of martial arts.

He met and studied with Sokaku Takeda, a master of *aiki-jutsu*, a form of swordsmanship. Morihei introduced many of the moves from sword fighting into the system he later named aikido.

Morihei once hoped he could teach his system of martial arts in China as a step to world peace. In 1924, Morihei went to China with the religious leader, Onisaburo. They wanted to organize Asian religious groups to oppose all wars. The Chinese warlords arrested them and bound Morihei in leg irons. Police then took him to an execution ground to be shot. Just before the execution was to take place, a Japanese government official got him released.

When he returned to Japan, Morihei taught aiki-jutsu. This was an early form of what later became aikido. He opened his own *dojo,* or school, and became a well-known teacher.

Until Japan entered World War II in 1941, Morihei gave special lessons to police, actors, dancers and sumo wrestlers. He changed the name of his system to *aiki-budo.*

In 1942 Morihei first used the word "aikido." The new name indicated Morihei's increased emphasis on mental or spiritual discipline.

An aikido master watches as students practice.

In this painting, Morihei Ueshiba demonstrates proper stance for kendo, or swordsmanship. He uses the same stance in aikido.

6

THE AIKIDO SHRINE AT

IWAMA

Aikido almost disappeared during World War II. Before the war, the Japanese government declared that all martial arts would be ruled by one agency. Morihei Ueshiba responded by moving out of Tokyo to the countryside. He took up farming. He also built a shrine to aikido at Iwama, just north of Tokyo.

Morihei lived a simple life in a two-room farmhouse with a dirt floor. He was more interested in spiritual matters than the comforts of a fine home. He wanted to live in harmony with nature. People who visited Morihei were startled by his shabby house, especially since he was not poor.

Morihei dedicated the aikido shrine at Iwama to the 43 gods he believed gave aikido its power. On his farm, he established an outdoor dojo. Before long he built an indoor dojo because so many students came to study with him.

For three years after the war, the shrine and the dojo on Morihei's farm preserved aikido. During that time, the Allied Occupation Forces that governed Japan forbade any teaching of martial arts. Because he lived in isolation, Morihei managed to teach aikido in spite of the law. He moved his dojo back to Tokyo after the war.

Here, the founder of aikido tends his garden near the aikido shrine at Iwama.

7

OTHER NAMES

Morihei Ueshiba had three sons. Two died in childhood. The third, Kisshomaru Ueshiba, succeeded his father as master at the Hombu dojo in Tokyo and became world leader of the art of aikido as Morihei had developed it.

As a boy, Kisshomaru Ueshiba was more interested in being a scholar than practicing aikido. As an adult, though, he became a master of aikido techniques. He also brought his scholarship to the world of aikido through his writing. After writing a biography of his father, Kisshomaru wrote *The Spirit of Aikido*. This book is an explanation of the spiritual meanings in aikido. It also tells about basic aikido techniques.

It is customary among many branches of martial arts for a person who has mastered the techniques to develop some of his own. Following this practice, several of Morihei Ueshiba's students have gone on to establish somewhat different forms of aikido.

IN AIKIDO

A master of Tomiki aikido demonstrates a throw.

An aikido master teaches how to hold a wrist lock. The student is about to slap the mat to signal he is beginning to feel pain so the master will release him.

Tomiki Kenji, one of Morihei's students, developed Tomiki aikido, a martial art practiced today in many cities in Japan and the United States.

Other schools, or forms, of aikido include the Yoshinkai, established by master Gozo Shioda, and the Yoseikan, developed by master Minoru Mochizuki.

Many aikidoists prefer to study aikido as it was developed by master Morihei Ueshiba. This school of aikido is called Aikikai So Hombu.

8

ETHICS

OF FIGHTING IN AIKIDO

In an ideal world, no one would ever attack anyone else. However in our world, where sometimes violent people attack others, the aikidoist is prepared to avoid injury.

Aikidoists practice their art for several reasons. They do so in order to keep the body in shape. They exercise as a form of relaxation, as a way to soothe the spirit and avoid stress. They practice in order to maintain skills in self-defense.

Self-defense is proper, says the teaching of aikido. Attack or making someone else angry enough to attack is not proper. Aikido judges fighting according to how justified each fight is.

An aikido student practices falling. Aikidoists learn to turn a fall into a roll to avoid injury.

In aikido throws, the aikidoist maintains his own balance by concentrating upon circular motions.

Aikido teaches that fighting, except in self-defense, is wrong. If someone attacks you with no provocation, it is considered ethical or proper to defend yourself. However, it is wrong to respond to an unprovoked fight by looking out only for yourself. Your defense must be one that does not cause permanent injury to the attacker. According to aikido teaching, it is wrong to cause serious injury, even in self-defense. Your defense should disable the attacker and allow you to leave the scene without receiving injury.

Aikido also teaches it is wrong both to attack without being attacked, and it is wrong to tease someone into attacking. Doing either would be an abuse of aikido teaching.

A NONCOMPETITIVE SYSTEM OF

D E F E N S E

Master Morihei Ueshiba, the founder of aikido, said that aikido should never become a competitive sport. He opposed tournaments and contests. He disliked emphasis on ranking according to numbers of wins, and he scorned giving trophies. For there to be a winner, there must be a loser. Master Ueshiba objected to the harm done to both. Losing can harm the human spirit, he said, and winning encourages disregard for others.

Anyone seeing an aikido demonstration for the first time might think the circular movements look more like a dance than a fighting art. Those expecting yells, punches and high kicks will be disappointed. However, aikido is effective. A person trained in aikido will know how to overcome an attacker who kicks and punches.

Aikido students learn to put pressure on joints to disable an attacker.

There are no tournaments in aikido. Students learn the art as a means of self-discipline and for self-defense.

Movements in aikido are based upon circular motions and on control of balance. Aikidoists study ways to focus mental and physical powers both for self-defense and for becoming at peace with themselves.

Aikido students do not learn to attack. They learn to respond to an attack. An important goal of a person trained in aikido is to stop violence without causing serious injury to the attacker.

One special move that black belts in aikido have mastered is throwing an attacker with a knife to the ground, while at the same time taking the knife away.

10

AIKIDO AS A

DEFENSIVE

ART

Aikidoists never attack. They respond to attacks. Aikido teaches you all the ways an attacker might come at you. An attacker might come armed or unarmed, so aikido has ways of dealing with both.

There are two stages in an unarmed attack. The first is the attacker's movement toward the victim. The second is what aikidoists call the technical stage. It involves recognizing the kind of attack – for example, a grab, a punch or a kick. Aikido teaches you to begin your defense as soon as someone makes an aggressive move toward you.

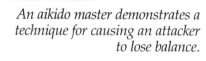

An aikido master demonstrates a technique for causing an attacker to lose balance.

Your goal is to throw the attacker off-balance while maintaining your own stability. Balance is basic to aikido defense.

It is hard to unbalance a person who is standing still. However, it is easy to do so if the person is moving. If an attacker is rushing toward you, wait until the last moment, step aside, and push the attacker. This will cause him to fall. The faster the person is moving, the easier it is to unbalance him. This also means that the slower a person is moving, the more difficult it is to cause him to fall.

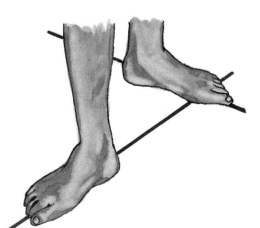

The basic foot stance in aikido helps the aikidoist stay balanced.

The founder of aikido, Morihei Ueshiba, continued teaching aikido even as a very old man.

The circular movements in aikido allow you to redirect the attacker's movements, causing him to fall while you remain standing. It takes hours of practice to learn the movements so you do not injure yourself or the attacker.

11

SHIHO-NIGE

THE BASIC THROW IN AIKIDO

Kisshomaru Ueshiba, the son of the founder of aikido, calls *shiho-nige* the beginning and end of aikido technique. Shiho-nige is a way of throwing an attacker that all beginners learn.

Knowing shiho-nige well is a sign of being an expert.

Shiho-nige involves stepping out and turning while taking an attacker's wrist. The aikidoist then lifts the wrist, turns, and throws the attacker by swinging down.

The founder of aikido taught that every move in shiho-nige is similar to moves in a sword fight. Think of your hand and an attacker's hand as swords. Meet the attacker's sword (hand) with yours. Step left, turn, step right. Lift your sword (hand) over your head, drawing with it the wrist of the attacker. Chop down.

An aikido master demonstrates shiho-nige, a basic throw taught to beginners.

Your circular motion will draw the attacker's motion into yours. You will remain balanced while the attacker will lean out of balance. When you "chop" down while holding the attacker's wrist, he will flip completely out of balance.

Shiho-nige, like many aikido moves, can be dangerous if done wrong. It can injure both doer and attacker. It is important to remember that aikido teaches that you should not injure an attacker. No one should try learning shiho-nige without guidance from an aikido master.

12

EARNING

A
B
E
L
T

IN
AIKIDO

Like other martial arts, aikido recognizes expertise by awarding belts. However, there is no standard of colors in aikido for those below black belt. In some aikido clubs, everyone who has not earned a black belt wears a white one. Other clubs recognize training stages with belts of different colors.

There are six ranks of beginner, called *kyu*. In most aikido clubs, the lowest five kyu ranks wear a white belt. Those in the highest kyu rank wear a brown belt. An expert is called *dan* and wears a black belt.

In many clubs in Europe and the United States, the belt colors for kyu change with each rank. The kyu colors, from least to most experience, are white, yellow, orange, green, blue and brown.

A teacher performs kokyn-nage, *a technique for throwing an attacker.*

An aikido master teaches a way to disarm an attacker who has a knife. Here, the master wears a blue hakima. Traditional hakimas are black, but some schools accept blue ones.

Most clubs recognize nine degrees of dan, or black belt. Earning a black belt requires a person to know advanced aikido techniques. These techniques include being able to stop an attack from several people at once.

In aikido, as in other martial arts, people wishing to earn a higher standing in kyu or dan must practice in the dojo for a set number of hours and learn a set number of techniques. For example, some aikido clubs require 40 hours of practice and mastery of four basic moves in order to hold the lowest rank of kyu.

13

WHAT IS
T
R
U
E
AIKIDO?

A number of students who learned from the founder of aikido have started their own schools. These teach aikido techniques in different ways. So it might be logical to ask, "What is the true aikido? Whose methods are the correct ones?"

The answer to these questions is that there is not one exact way to perform any of the aikido techniques. All people move in slightly different ways. Even an aikido master continues to refine techniques. Refining means change.

Masters who have started their own forms of aikido teach aikido moves as they understand them. These masters know that some of their students will become masters. Some of them will go on to establish their own schools of aikido. The new schools will no doubt teach techniques in slightly different ways.

Many techniques in aikido were adapted from ancient Japanese sword fighting.

Aikidoists learn to meet an attack with open hands, not with fists.

Aikido masters say that after years of practice, they still learn more about even basic techniques. Master Shirata Rinjiro said that after 50 years, he was finally understanding how to perform shiho-nige, a basic technique taught to beginners.

There is no one true way to perform aikido. To be aikidoists, people need to adhere to the nonviolent ideals of the founder. They also need to learn aikido moves and adapt them to their own body movements.

14

AIKIDO

TODAY

Hundreds of thousands of people in over 40 countries have studied aikido. Most aikidoists practice because it relaxes them and keeps them in good physical shape. Many learn the art in order to defend themselves if attacked. Others, such as dancers and models, find aikido helps them move with more grace. Some find a kind of spiritual peace in aikido practice. Certainly the founder of aikido hoped his art would be useful to make the aikidoist at peace with self and others.

Because it appeals to many people for many reasons, the study of aikido continues to grow around the world.

This aikido move begins with a sweeping, circular motion and ends with a wrist lock.

abacus: a device made of beads designed for performing basic arithmetic.

aikido: a Japanese word meaning "the way of harmony with ki"; the term refers to a system of martial arts first developed by Morihei Ueshiba.

aikidoist: one who studies or practices aikido.

aiki-jutsu: a form of kendo, or Japanese swordsmanship.

Aikikai So Hombu: the form of aikido developed by Master Morihei Ueshiba.

dan: a ranking in martial arts acknowledged with the awarding of a black belt.

dojo: a school or a place where people study martial arts.

hakima: black or blue pants worn over a white martial arts uniform by aikidoists. The hakima is also used by schools of kendo, or Japanese swordsmen.

jujitsu: a form of traditional Japanese martial arts characterized by grappling and body throws.

kendo: Japanese swordsmanship.

kokyn-nage: an aikido technique for throwing an attacker.

kyu: one of the six ranks of beginners in aikido.

martial arts: any form of military training; often the term refers to empty-handed fighting, as well as to the various forms of exercises and sports developed from ancient fighting skills.

samurai: a class of elite Japanese warriors who for hundreds of years fought the battles of emperors and warlords.

shiho-nige: the first body throw learned by beginning aikido students.

sumo wrestling: an ancient form of Japanese martial arts, now a popular sport in Japan.

Tomiki aikido: a form of aikido developed by Tomiki Kenji, once a student of Morihei Ueshiba.

Yoseikan aikido: a form of aikido developed by Minoru Mochizuki.

Yoshinkai aikido: a form of aikido developed by Gozo Shioda.

INDEX